This Book Belongs to

_____

a Scientist in Training

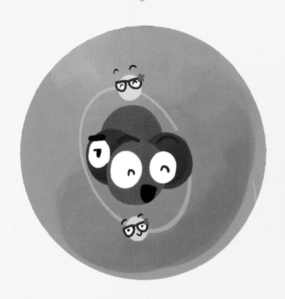
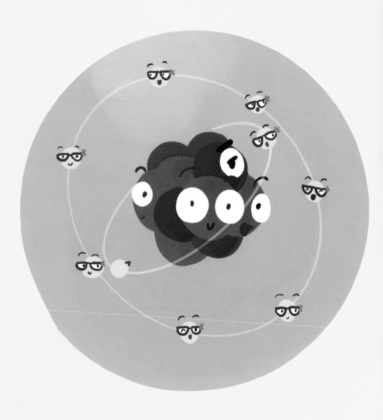

Say hello to the atoms that build everything you see.

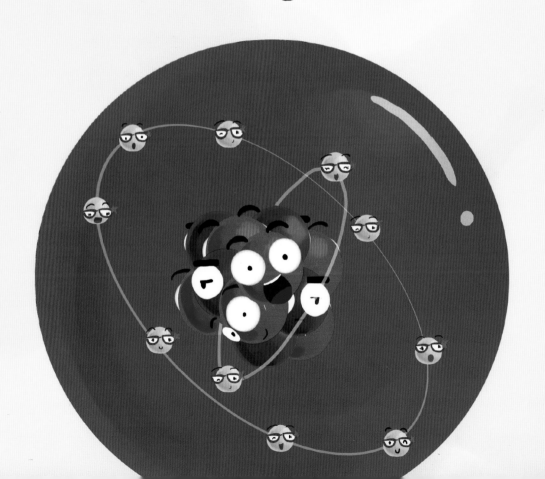

Your hands, this book, the air, giraffes, and every single tree.

MY FIRST SCIENCE TEXTBOOK

Atoms

Created and Edited by John J. Coveyou
Written by Mary Wissinger
Illustrated by Harriet Kim Anh Rodis

If you want to make an atom, the recipe starts with protons and neutrons.

Squish them together, use high heat, and sprinkle in electrons.

The strong force holds the nucleus tight, while electrons get to race.

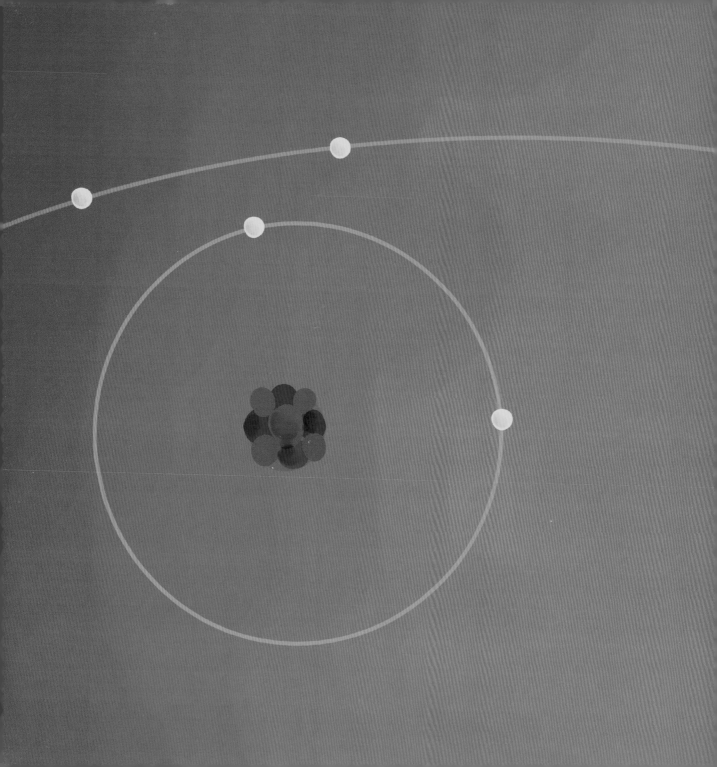

They fly so far from the nucleus that atoms are mostly empty space.

When atoms get together, electrons are for sharing and taking.

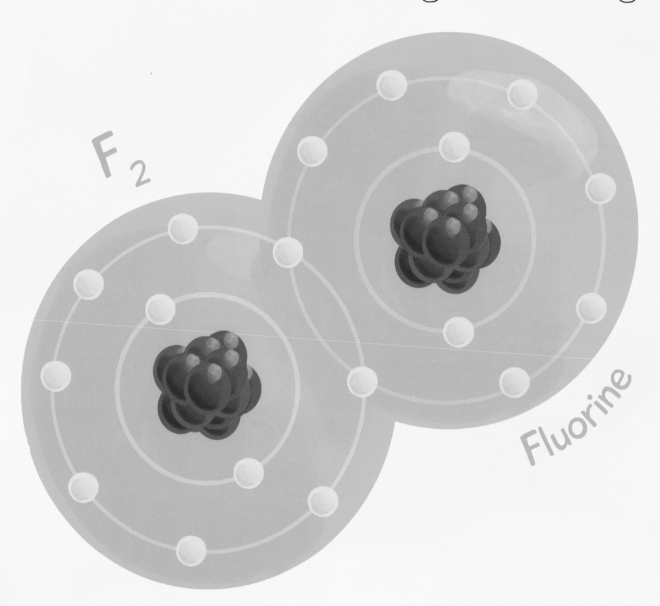

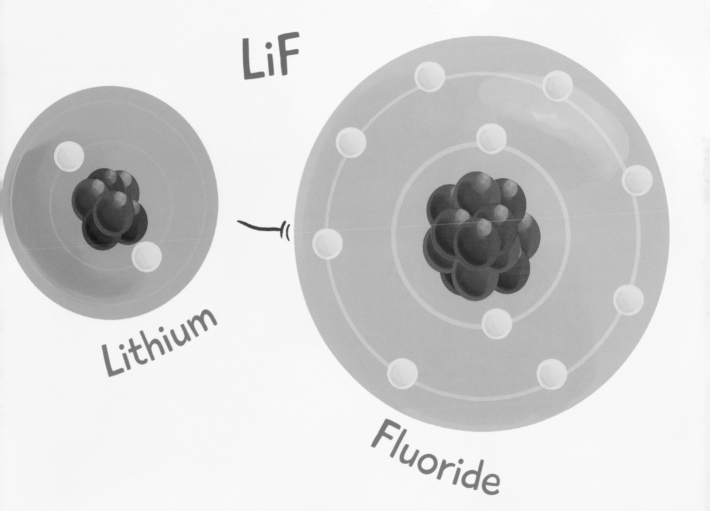

These covalent and ionic bonds are molecules in the making.

Covalent Bond

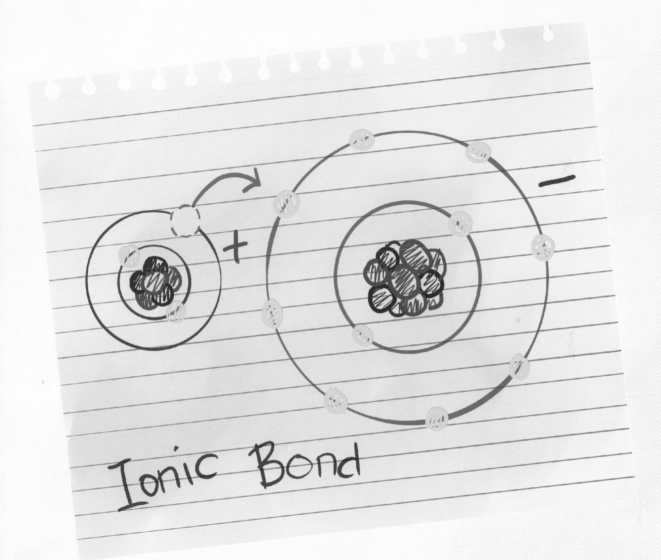

Ionic Bond

There is a special word for when atoms look and act the same.

It's called an element, and each element has a name.

Elements go in increasing order on the Periodic Table.

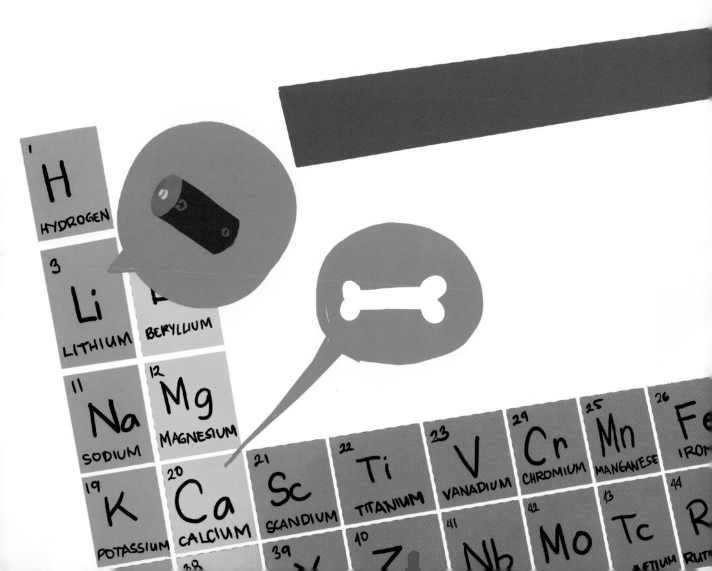

Atoms compose each tiny speck
from here to distant stars.

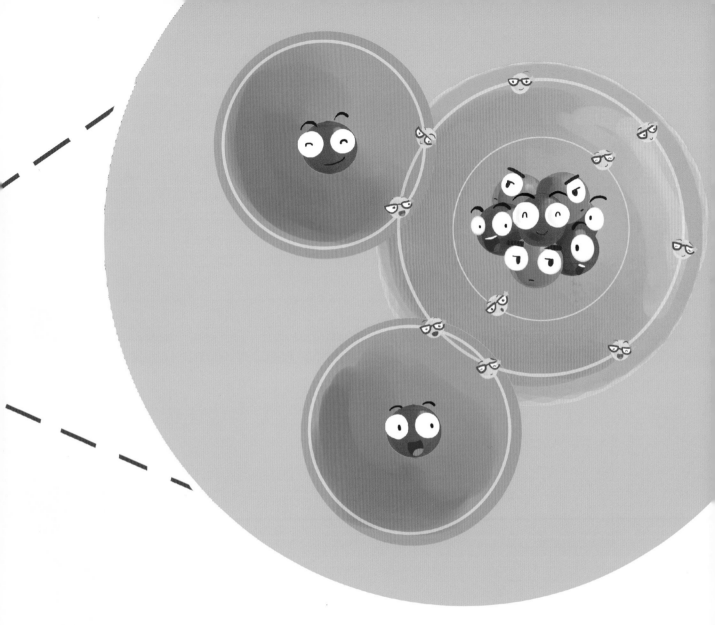

You contain galaxies of atoms, so protons, neutrons, and electrons, too.

You live in the universe,
and a universe lives in you.

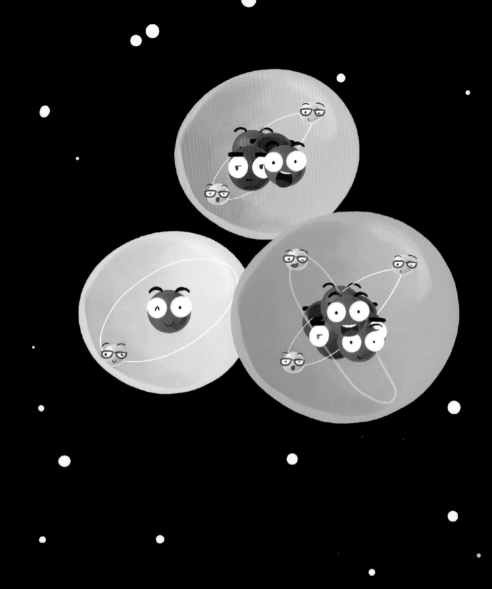